SCALING UP

STRATEGIES FOR GROWING A BUSINESS FROM $1 MILLION TO $10 MILLION

KEVIN STANLEY

Copyright © 2024 by Kevin Stanley

All rights reserved. No part of this book may be reproduced, stored in a retrieval system, or transmitted in any form or by any means, electronic, mechanical, photocopying, recording, or otherwise, without the prior written permission of the author.

Table of contents

INTRODUCTION — 5
AN OVERVIEW OF THE CHALLENGES INVOLVED IN GROWING A BUSINESS AND THE PROCESS OF SCALING Up — 5
CHAPTER 1 — 15
PREPARATION — 15
- Assessing Your Business Readiness for Scaling — 15
- Defining Your Vision and Goals for Scaling — 21
- Building a Strong Foundation: Systems, Processes, and Culture — 29

CHAPTER 2 — 39
TEAM AND LEADERSHIP — 39
- Building a Scalable Leadership Team — 39
- Developing a Strong Management Structure — 46
- Attracting and Retaining Top Talent — 54

CHAPTER 3 — 65
MARKETING AND SALES — 65
- Scaling Your Marketing Strategy — 65
- Playbooks and Processes for Creating a Sales Machine — 72
- Using Technology in Marketing and Sales — 79

CHAPTER 4 — 91
OPERATIONS AND EFFICIENCY — 91
- Streamlining Operations for Scalability — 91
- Putting in Place Effective Procedures and Systems — 100

Financial Planning and Cash Flow Management 109
CHAPTER 5   121
GROWTH AND EXPANSION   121
Identifying New Markets and Opportunities 121
Cooperative and Strategic Alliances 129
Acquisitions and Mergers: Growth Strategies 138
CHAPTER 6   149
OVERCOMING OBSTACLES   149
Handling Scaling Difficulties and Growth Pains 149
Preserving Culture and Principles in the Face of Fast Development 157
Managing Uncertainty and Change 163
CONCLUSION   171

INTRODUCTION

AN OVERVIEW OF THE CHALLENGES INVOLVED IN GROWING A BUSINESS AND THE PROCESS OF SCALING Up

It is a transforming journey that involves more than just vision and hard work to grow a firm from one million dollars in sales to ten million dollars in revenue. It needs a deliberate approach, a sturdy structure, and the capacity to navigate through numerous problems that might develop along the way. Building a sustainable and resilient business that is able to weather changes in the market, adapt to changing consumer wants, and keep its competitive edge is the goal of scaling up. Scaling up is not only about raising revenue or expanding operations.

In this introduction, we will examine the notion of scaling up, explain the primary obstacles firms encounter during this important development period, and set the scene for the methods that will be discussed in the coming chapters. Whether you are an entrepreneur who wants to take your startup to the next level or a seasoned business owner who wants to grow your company's presence, it is essential for your success to have a solid grasp of these core principles.

The Concept of Scaling Up

In order to scale up a firm, it is necessary to expand in a manner that will boost income while simultaneously controlling expenses and difficulties. The goal is to grow your company's operations so that you can manage a bigger market share, a greater number of clients, and higher sales volumes without sacrificing quality or efficiency. This procedure is quite different from the early phase of the startup process, which is often centered on ensuring survival, validating the market, and determining whether or not the product is a good match for the market.

At its heart, scaling up involves a change in mentality and strategy. In order to successfully establish a team that is capable of putting the company's vision into action, entrepreneurs need to make the move from being active in every part of the firm. Putting in place the methods and procedures that will enable the company to continue to function in a smooth and effective manner, even as it expands, is a necessary step. Moreover, scaling up involves a strategic emphasis on long-term objectives, resource allocation, and risk management.

The Most Important Obstacles to Scaling Up

While the promise of establishing a company is thrilling, it comes with a distinct set of hurdles. Understanding and predicting these problems may help entrepreneurs design methods to overcome them and achieve sustainable development.

Leadership and Team Development: One of the most critical hurdles in scaling up is developing a leadership team that can drive the company's development. This requires not just acquiring the appropriate personnel but also developing current staff to take on greater responsibility. As the firm expands, the founder's position changes, and it becomes necessary to delegate efficiently and enable others to lead.

Preserving Company Culture: As the team increases, preserving the company culture that made the organization prosper in its early stages might be tough. A great culture stimulates employee engagement, drives performance, and attracts top talent. Ensuring that the company's values and objectives are preserved, even when new people come on board, is vital for long-term success.

Financial Management: Managing funds during a growth period is challenging. Businesses need to invest in new technology, infrastructure, and personnel while ensuring they have the cash flow to function effectively. This demands precise financial planning, budgeting, and frequently attracting external finance or investment.

Operational Efficiency: Scaling up frequently means boosting manufacturing capacity, simplifying operations, and improving supply networks. This may be tough since it demands firms to enhance their processes, implement new technology, and guarantee that their operations can manage greater demand without sacrificing quality.

Market Expansion: Expanding into new markets, whether geographical or demographic, is a critical growth strategy. However, it comes with dangers such as knowing local rules, cultural differences, and competitive landscapes. A detailed market study and a well-thought-out entrance plan are important to minimize these dangers.

Client Retention and Acquisition: Growing a client base while maintaining current customers is a balancing act. Businesses must continually innovate and enhance their services to attract new clients while delivering outstanding service to keep current ones. Customer feedback and data analytics play a key role in understanding customer requirements and preferences.

Technology and Innovation: Leveraging technology to generate growth is crucial. This involves adopting new technologies for customer relationship management (CRM), enterprise resource planning (ERP), and marketing automation. Staying ahead of technical trends and investing in innovation may create a competitive edge and enable scalable development.

Risk Management: Scaling up exposes firms to additional risks, including operational, financial, and market risks. Developing a strong risk management approach that includes contingency planning, insurance, and frequent risk assessments will help minimize these risks and maintain company continuity.

Setting the Stage for Strategic Growth

The journey from $1 million to $10 million in sales is a pivotal time that may determine the destiny of a corporation. It demands a strategic approach where every action is linked to the long-term objectives of the organization. In the following chapters, we will look further into the strategies and approaches that may help firms overcome the hurdles listed above and achieve sustainable development.

We will study themes such as:

Building a Scalable Business Model: Understanding the Fundamental Components of a Scalable Business Model and How to Develop One That Supports Growth.

Leadership and Organizational Development: Strategies for constructing a high-performing leadership team and developing a resilient organizational structure.

Financial Planning and Management: Best Practices for Managing Money, Procuring Financing, and Guaranteeing Financial Stability Throughout Expansion.

Operational Excellence: Techniques for Optimizing Operations, Enhancing Efficiency, and Using Technology to Promote Scalability.

Market Penetration and Expansion: Approaches for entering new markets, analyzing client segmentation, and implementing efficient marketing strategies.

Customer-Centric Growth: How to balance customer acquisition and retention, increase customer experience, and establish a loyal customer base.

Innovation and Adaptability: The significance of developing a culture of innovation, keeping ahead of industry trends, and being adaptive to change.

By the conclusion of this book, you will have a complete grasp of what it takes to expand a firm effectively. You will be prepared with practical ideas, tangible tactics, and real-world examples that may assist you on your development path. Scaling up is not a simple undertaking, but with the correct mentality, tools, and techniques, it is feasible. Let's go on this adventure together and uncover the potential of your company.

CHAPTER 1

PREPARATION

Assessing Your Business Readiness for Scaling

Before going on the path to expand your company from $1 million to $10 million, it's vital to analyze if your organization is ready for such development. Scaling isn't just about generating income; it entails strengthening your operations, upgrading your processes, and ensuring that your organization can manage the higher responsibilities that come with growth. This chapter will walk you through the process of analyzing your business's preparedness to grow, identifying possible vulnerabilities, and planning to handle them successfully.

Evaluating Your Current Business Model

The first stage in determining your preparedness for scaling is to review your present business model. Consider the following questions:

Is your company concept scalable? A scalable company model is one that can develop without being limited by its structure or available resources when confronted with growing production needs.

Do you have a clear value proposition? Your value proposition should clearly describe the distinct advantages your product or service gives to clients.

Is your income strategy sustainable? Assess if your income sources are varied and whether they can sustain expansion without substantial adjustments.

Financial Health Check

Financial stability is a vital component in establishing your preparedness to grow. Conduct a full financial health check, including:

Cash Flow Analysis: Ensure you have a positive cash flow and that you can handle rising operational expenditures.

Profit Margins: Assess your profit margins to see whether they are adequate to fund growing initiatives.

Debt Levels: Evaluate your present debt levels and ensure they are manageable as you grow.

Access to Capital: Consider your capacity to get extra money if required.

Operational Efficiency

Your operations need to be efficient and capable of managing growing volumes. volumes. volumes.

Evaluate Manufacturing Capacity: Determine whether your present manufacturing facilities and procedures can accommodate additional demand.

Supply network robustness: Assess the dependability and flexibility of your supply network.

Technology Infrastructure: Ensure that your technology infrastructure can sustain expansion, including your IT systems and digital tools.

Market Position and Customer Base

Understanding your market position and client base is critical for scaling...

Market Demand: Research if there is adequate demand for your product or service to sustain expansion.

Competitive Landscape: Analyze your competitors and find your competitive advantages.

Customer Loyalty and Satisfaction: Assess your present customer satisfaction levels and loyalty, since maintaining existing customers is vital throughout growth periods.

Team and Leadership

Your team and leadership have a crucial impact on your capacity to scale...

Leadership Capabilities: Evaluate if your present leadership team has the skills and expertise to run a bigger, more complicated business.

Talent and Skills: Assess if you have the required talent and skills within your team to enable development.

Organizational Structure: Consider whether your organizational structure can scale effectively or if it requires revamping.

Risk Assessment

Identify any hazards that might harm your scaling efforts:

Operational Risks: Consider risks connected to manufacturing, the supply chain, and technology.

Financial Risks: Assess risks connected to cash flow, finance, and financial management.

Market Risks: Evaluate risks linked with market demand, competition, and consumer preferences.

Regulatory Risks: Consider any regulatory or compliance challenges that might hinder your development.

SWOT Analysis

Conduct a SWOT analysis to determine your business's strengths, weaknesses, opportunities, and threats. This study will help you understand your internal capabilities and external environment, offering a thorough assessment of your preparedness to grow.

By properly examining your business's preparation for growth, you may find areas that need improvement and take proactive efforts to fix them. This planning will create the basis for a successful scaling journey.

Defining Your Vision and Goals for Scaling

With a firm knowledge of your business's readiness to grow, the next stage is to articulate your vision and set precise targets for scaling. A well-defined vision and clear objectives will give direction, motivation, and a framework for monitoring progress.

Crafting Your Vision Statement

Your vision statement should reflect what you intend to accomplish as you expand your firm. It should be:

Inspiring: Your vision should motivate and inspire your staff, stakeholders, and consumers.

Clear and Concise: It should be simple to comprehend and remember.

Future-Focused: Your vision should represent your long-term objectives and the effect you plan to create in your sector.

Setting SMART Goals

SMART objectives are specific, measurable, achievable, relevant, and time-bound. Setting SMART objectives can help you build a clear plan for scaling:

explicit: Define clear and explicit objectives. For example, "Increase annual revenue to $10 million within three years."

quantifiable: Ensure your objectives are quantifiable so you can measure progress. For example, "Achieve a 25% annual growth rate."

Achievable: Set realistic objectives based on your present skills and resources.

Relevant: Ensure your objectives connect with your overarching vision and company plan.

Time-bound: Set timelines for attaining your objectives. For example, "Expand to three new markets within two years."

Aligning Your Team

Your team has to be aligned with your vision and objectives to guarantee coherent efforts towards scaling...

Explain the Vision: Clearly explain your vision and objectives to your staff. Ensure they understand the relevance of these objectives and how their responsibilities contribute to accomplishing them.

Promote Buy-In: Involve your staff in the goal-setting process to promote buy-in and commitment. Encourage input and ensure they feel appreciated and heard.

Set departmental objectives: Break down your overall objectives into departmental goals. This will help each team understand their individual contributions and responsibilities.

Developing a Strategic Plan

A strategic plan includes the activities and actions necessary to attain your vision and goals:

Market study: Conduct a detailed market study to identify growth prospects and possible constraints.

Competitive plan: Develop a plan to separate your firm from rivals and grab market share.

Resource Allocation: Plan how you will distribute resources, including cash, staff, and technology, to support your growth efforts.

Milestones and Metrics: Define essential milestones and metrics to measure your progress. Regularly analyze these indicators to measure your performance and make the required modifications.

Building a Resilient Business Model

A resilient business model can adapt to changes and endure challenges..

Diversify Revenue Sources: Diversify your revenue sources to lessen dependence on a single source of income.

Enhance Flexibility: Build flexibility into your operations and procedures to adjust swiftly to market changes.

Focus on Innovation: Foster a culture of innovation to continually enhance your goods, services, and processes.

Leveraging Technology

Technology plays a key role in growing a business..

Invest in Scalable Technology: Invest in technology that can expand with your company, such as cloud-based solutions and scalable software.

Automation: Implement automation to simplify operations, decrease manual effort, and boost efficiency.

Data Analytics: Utilize data analytics to make educated choices, evaluate consumer behavior, and find growth prospects.

Building Strategic Partnerships

Strategic relationships may bring extra resources, knowledge, and market access.

Identify Potential Partners: Identify firms that match your products and share your mission.

Negotiate win-win agreements: develop collaborations that benefit both parties and coincide with your growth ambitions.

Leverage Partner Networks: Utilize your partners' networks to broaden your market reach and boost your skills.

Defining your vision and creating clear objectives for scaling will create a strong basis for your development journey. By aligning your team, formulating a strategic strategy, and using technology and partnerships, you can start your organization on the path to realizing its growing objectives.

Building a Strong Foundation: Systems, Processes, and Culture

Having evaluated your business's preparedness and outlined your vision and objectives, the next stage is to construct a firm foundation. This requires developing sturdy systems and procedures and fostering a culture that fosters development. A solid foundation is vital for guaranteeing that your organization can withstand the complexity and difficulties of expanding.

Establishing Efficient Systems and Processes

Efficient systems and procedures are the backbone of a scalable firm. They provide stability, efficiency, and quality as your firm grows.

Standard Operating Procedures (SOPs): Develop thorough SOPs for all important operations. These practices should be recorded and immediately available to your staff.

Workflow Automation: Identify repeated processes and automate them to boost productivity and decrease the chance of mistakes. Automation solutions may simplify procedures like billing, customer relationship management (CRM), and inventory management.

Performance Monitoring: Implement performance monitoring systems to measure important indicators and verify that your operations are working effectively. Regularly evaluate these numbers to discover opportunities for improvement.

Investing in Technology Infrastructure

A solid technological infrastructure is crucial for enabling expansion and guaranteeing operational efficiency.

Scalable IT Solutions: Invest in IT solutions that can grow with your organization, such as cloud computing and software-as-a-service (SaaS) platforms.

Data Management: Implement a complete data management system to store, organize, and analyze data. This will provide vital information for decision-making and help you uncover development prospects.

Cybersecurity: Ensure that your technological infrastructure is safe and that you have mechanisms in place to guard against cyber attacks.

Enhancing Operational Capabilities

Enhancing your operational skills will help you fulfill rising demand and sustain high standards of quality:

Capacity Planning: Assess your present capacity and prepare for future expansion. This may require expanding your manufacturing facilities, growing your workers, or outsourcing specific activities.

Supply Chain Optimization: Optimize your supply chain to guarantee dependability and flexibility. Build connections with important suppliers and build contingency plans to reduce hazards.

Quality Control: Implement stringent quality control methods to maintain high standards as you grow. Regularly assess and update these steps to ensure they stay effective.

Fostering a Strong Company Culture

A strong corporate culture is vital for recruiting and keeping top individuals, driving performance, and supporting growth.

Establish Core Values: Clearly establish your core values and ensure they are interwoven into all elements of your company. These ideals should influence your decision-making and conduct.

Express Vision and Objectives: Regularly express your vision and objectives to your team. Ensure that they understand their role in accomplishing these objectives and how their job contributes to the overall success of the firm.

Employee Engagement: Foster a culture of engagement by including workers in decision-making, giving chances for growth and development, and recognizing and rewarding their efforts.

Diversity and Inclusion: Promote diversity and inclusion inside your company. Diverse teams provide various views and ideas, which may stimulate innovation and better decision-making.

Building a High-Performing Leadership Team

A high-performing leadership team is critical for driving growth and handling the complexity of scaling.

Leadership Development: Invest in leadership development programs to increase the skills and capacities of your leadership team. Provide chances for training, mentoring, and coaching.

Delegation and Empowerment: Empower your leaders to make choices and take ownership of their areas of responsibility. Effective delegation is vital for managing a developing firm.

Cross-functional cooperation: Encourage cross-functional cooperation to ensure that diverse departments work together towards similar objectives. This will promote communication, cooperation, and problem-solving.

Financial Management and Planning

Effective financial management and planning are vital for ensuring the sustainability of your growth.

Budgeting and Forecasting: Develop precise budgets and financial projections to prepare for future development. Regularly examine and revise your projections to reflect changes in your company's environment.

Cost Control: Implement cost control strategies to manage expenditures and assure profitability. This may entail negotiating better terms with suppliers, minimizing waste, and enhancing operational efficiency.

Financing and Investment: Explore numerous financing possibilities to help your development, such as venture capital, private equity, or bank loans. Ensure that you have a clear strategy for how you will utilize this cash to meet your scaling objectives.

Continuous Improvement and Innovation

Continuous improvement and innovation are crucial to remaining competitive and generating growth.

Process Improvement: Regularly examine and improve your procedures to boost efficiency, quality, and customer happiness. Use approaches such as Lean, Six Sigma, or Total Quality Management (TQM) to guide your efforts.

Innovation Culture: Foster a culture of innovation by encouraging workers to discuss ideas, experiment with new ways, and take measured risks. Provide resources and assistance for innovative efforts.

consumer input: Use consumer input to find areas for improvement and innovation. Regularly communicate with your consumers to learn about their wants and preferences and implement their ideas into your product and service development.

Building a solid foundation via efficient procedures and processes, robust technological infrastructure, and a supportive business culture is key to successful growth. By investing in these areas, you can establish a resilient company that is well-equipped to manage the difficulties and possibilities of expansion.

CHAPTER 2

TEAM AND LEADERSHIP

Building a Scalable Leadership Team

Scaling a firm from $1 million to $10 million involves more than just a sound business strategy and operational efficiency; it demands a scalable leadership team capable of steering the company through its development trajectory. A scalable leadership team is not only proficient at managing present operations but also ready to foresee and negotiate the problems of growth. This chapter will discuss the essential factors required in developing a leadership team that can support and drive your business's scaling initiatives.

Understanding the Role of Leadership in Scaling

Leadership plays a crucial part in the scaling process. Effective leaders:

Set Vision and Strategy: Leaders establish a clear vision and build strategies to attain development goals.

Drive Culture and Values: Leaders infuse the company's values and culture into all elements of the business, generating a cohesive and motivated workforce.

Make strategic choices: Leaders make educated choices that balance short-term requirements with long-term aspirations.

Manage Change: Leaders steer the organization through changes, ensuring seamless transitions and minimal interruptions.

Identifying Leadership Gaps and Needs

Before developing a scalable leadership team, it's vital to identify present gaps and future needs.

Skill Gaps: Assess the present skills within your leadership team and identify any gaps that might limit progress.

Experience Gaps: Determine if your existing executives have the experience required to run a bigger, more complicated company.

Role Gaps: Identify additional leadership positions that may be essential as the firm expands, such as heads of new divisions or regional managers.

Recruiting Leaders with the Right Skills and Mindset

Recruiting executives that possess the requisite

abilities and development attitude is crucial for scaling:

describe key abilities: Clearly describe the abilities necessary for each leadership function, such as strategic thinking, operational knowledge, and change management.

Look for Growth Mentality: Seek leaders who have a growth mentality, are open to learning, and can adapt to changing situations.

Diversity and Inclusion: Promote diversity within your leadership team to introduce various viewpoints and improve decision-making.

Developing Leadership Capabilities

Developing the competencies of your leadership team is a continual process.

Training and Development: Invest in leadership training programs that concentrate on skills essential for scaling, such as strategic planning, financial management, and team development.

Mentoring and Coaching: Provide chances for mentoring and coaching to assist leaders in building their abilities and obtaining insights from experienced mentors.

Leadership Programs: Create internal leadership development programs to discover and nurture emerging leaders inside your business.

Delegating Effectively

Effective delegation is vital for growth since it enables leaders to concentrate on strategic efforts while allowing others to handle operational tasks.

Outline duties and responsibilities: Clearly outline the duties and responsibilities of each leader to eliminate overlap and assure accountability.

Empower Leaders: Empower your leaders to make choices and take control of their areas of responsibility.

Trust and assistance: Build trust among your leadership team by giving assistance and resources required to succeed.

Building a Cohesive Leadership Team

A cohesive leadership team works together towards similar goals:

Foster cooperation: Encourage cooperation and communication among leaders to guarantee alignment and coordination.

Frequent Meetings: Hold frequent leadership meetings to review progress, handle difficulties, and prepare for the future.

Conflict Resolution: Develop processes for resolving disputes and ensuring that differences are handled constructively.

Succession Planning

Succession planning guarantees that your leadership team stays strong and stable as the firm grows.

Identify Successors: Identify possible successors for important leadership positions and give them growth opportunities.

Cross-Training: Implement cross-training programs to ensure that executives have a comprehensive grasp of many sectors of the organization.

Continuity Plans: Develop continuity plans to facilitate a seamless transition in the case of leadership changes.

By developing a scalable leadership team, you

can guarantee that your organization has the strategic direction, cultural alignment, and operational supervision required to sustain growth. Investing in leadership development, effective delegation, and succession planning can help establish a resilient leadership team capable of taking your firm to new heights.

Developing a Strong Management Structure

As your firm expands, establishing a robust management structure is vital to handling growing complexity, promoting efficiency, and ensuring good decision-making. A comprehensive management structure offers clarity in duties and responsibilities, improves communication, and supports strategic efforts. This chapter will lead you through the important components of creating a solid management structure to support your scaling efforts.

Defining Roles and Responsibilities

Clearly defined roles and duties are the cornerstone of an efficient management structure.

Position Clarity: Ensure that each management position is clearly defined, with precise duties and accountabilities.

Job Descriptions: Develop clear job descriptions for all management roles, describing important duties, performance goals, and reporting linkages.

Authority and responsibility: Establish clear lines of authority and responsibility to guarantee that managers can make choices and are accountable for results.

Organizational Structure

Choosing the correct organizational structure is crucial for enabling growth.

Functional Structure: organize the company by functions (e.g., marketing, finance, operations). This structure may improve specialization but may generate silos.

Divisional Structure: organize the company into divisions (e.g., product lines, geographical areas). This structure provides for flexibility and concentration on specialized markets but may lead to duplication of efforts.

Matrix Structure: Combines functional and divisional organizations with dual reporting lines. This structure may increase cooperation but may also produce complexity and misunderstanding.

Flat Structure: Reduces tiers of management, facilitates speedier decision-making, and increases employee empowerment. However, it may hinder the ability to manage a vast firm.

Communication Channels

Effective communication channels are vital for ensuring information flows easily across the organization.

Vertical Communication: Establish clear vertical communication routes to guarantee that information moves up and down the hierarchy effectively.

Horizontal Communication: Promote horizontal communication across departments to increase cooperation and coordination.

Frequent Updates: Implement frequent update meetings and reports to keep everyone informed about progress and difficulties.

Decision-Making Processes

Establishing good decision-making procedures is vital for retaining agility and responsiveness.

Decentralized Decision-Making: Empower managers to make decisions within their areas of responsibility to promote agility and responsiveness.

Explicit standards: Provide explicit standards and frameworks for decision-making to maintain consistency and alignment with the company's objectives.

Collaborative Decision-Making: Encourage collaborative decision-making procedures to exploit multiple viewpoints and expertise.

Performance Management

A thorough performance management system ensures that managers are aligned with the company's objectives and are responsible for their performance.

Goal Setting: Set clear, measurable goals for managers that match with the company's strategic objectives.

Frequent evaluations: Conduct frequent performance evaluations to measure progress, give comments, and identify growth needs.

Recognition and incentives: Implement recognition and incentive programs to promote and incentivize outstanding performance.

Talent Development

Investing in talent development is vital for developing a strong management structure.

Training Programs: Develop comprehensive training programs to develop the skills and capacities of your management.

Career tracks: Create clear career tracks to give managers chances for development and progress.

Mentoring and Coaching: Offer mentoring and coaching to assist managers in their growth and help them negotiate issues.

Leveraging Technology

Technology may boost the efficiency and effectiveness of your management structure.

Management Software: Utilize management software to simplify operations, boost communication, and improve decision-making.

Data Analytics: Leverage data analytics to obtain insights into performance, discover patterns, and make educated choices.

Collaboration Tools: Implement collaboration tools to improve communication and cooperation among management.

Continuous Improvement

Continuous development is vital for sustaining a solid management structure as your organization scales.

Feedback Mechanisms: Establish feedback mechanisms to get information from managers and workers on what's working and what needs improvement.

Process Optimization: Regularly examine and improve management processes to boost efficiency and effectiveness.

Innovation: Encourage innovation within the management team to explore new methods of enhancing operations and attaining objectives.

By building a robust management structure, you can guarantee that your organization has the essential foundation to sustain development. Clear roles and duties, excellent communication channels, strong decision-making procedures, and continual improvement initiatives will produce a resilient and efficient management structure capable of propelling your firm ahead.

Attracting and Retaining Top Talent

Attracting and maintaining excellent personnel is important for expanding your organization. As you develop, having the appropriate people in the right positions will help you execute your objectives successfully, generate innovation, and retain a competitive advantage. This chapter will discuss tactics for hiring and keeping outstanding personnel to help your growing efforts.

Building a Compelling Employer Brand

A strong employer brand recruits top talent by

showing your organization as an employer of choice:

Identify Your Brand: Clearly identify what makes your firm special, including your culture, values, and purpose.

Promote Your Brand: Use your website, social media, and job posts to promote your employer brand and emphasize what makes your organization a wonderful place to work.

Employee Testimonials: Share employee testimonials and success stories to give honest insights into what it's like to work at your organization.

Recruitment Strategies

Effective recruiting tactics are vital for acquiring top talent.

Targeted Job Posts: Create targeted job posts that clearly define the skills, experience, and attributes you're searching for.

Talent Networks: Build talent networks and maintain ties with possible applicants, even if they're not actively seeking a job.

Recruitment Agencies: Partner with recruitment agencies to access a bigger pool of applicants and utilize their experience in identifying top people.

Employee Referrals: Implement employee referral programs to encourage your staff to suggest excellent prospects from their networks.

Hiring for Culture Fit and Skills

Hiring the right people includes locating applicants that not only have the requisite abilities but also suit your corporate culture.

Behavioral Interviews: Use behavioral interviews to analyze candidates' congruence with your company's values and culture.

Skill Assessments: Implement skill assessments and practical exams to evaluate candidates' skills and ensure they have the requisite competencies.

Cultural Fit: Prioritize cultural fit in your recruiting selections to guarantee that new personnel will flourish in your corporate environment.

Onboarding and Integration

A robust onboarding procedure helps new personnel integrate comfortably and become productive quickly.

Orientation Programs: Develop orientation programs to acquaint new recruits with your company's culture, values, and expectations.

Training and Development: Provide initial training to equip new recruits with the information and skills they need to succeed.

Mentorship Programs: Assign mentors to new recruits to give advice, support, and help them navigate their new jobs.

Creating a Positive Work Environment

A pleasant work environment promotes employee happiness and retention.

Work-Life Balance: Promote work-life balance by giving flexible work arrangements and valuing employees' personal time.

Employee Wellbeing: Implement programs to enhance employee wellbeing, including mental health services, exercise programs, and wellness activities.

Engaging workplaces: Create engaging and comfortable workplaces that support cooperation and productivity.

Offering Competitive Compensation and

Benefits

Competitive wages and perks are vital for recruiting and maintaining top talent.

Market Research: Conduct market research to verify your remuneration packages are competitive with industry norms.

Comprehensive Benefits: Offer comprehensive benefits, including health insurance, retirement plans, and other incentives that are vital to your workers.

Performance-Based Incentives: Implement performance-based incentives, such as bonuses and stock options, to promote strong performance and align employees' interests with the company's objectives.

Career Development and Growth Opportunities

Providing professional development and advancement opportunities is vital for keeping top talent.

Professional Development: Invest in professional development programs, such as training classes, seminars, and conferences, to assist personnel in upgrading their abilities.

Career tracks: Create defined career tracks to give workers chances for progress and growth within the firm.

Promotions and Internal Mobility: Prioritize promotions and internal mobility to recognize and reward employees' efforts and give them new challenges and possibilities.

Fostering a Culture of Recognition and Appreciation

A culture of acknowledgment and gratitude enhances morale and retention.

Recognition Programs: Implement recognition programs to reward employees' accomplishments and efforts.

Frequent Feedback: Provide frequent feedback and praise to workers to demonstrate gratitude for their efforts and help them develop.

Celebrating Milestones: Celebrate milestones and triumphs, both large and small, to build a sense of community and shared accomplishment.

Employee Engagement and Satisfaction

High levels of employee engagement and satisfaction are crucial to keeping great talent.

Staff Surveys: Conduct frequent staff surveys to gain input and identify areas for improvement.

Open Communication: Foster open communication channels to help staff feel heard and appreciated.

Team Building: Organize team-building

activities and events to enhance connections and promote a pleasant work atmosphere.

Adapting to Changing Workforce Trends

Adapting to shifting workforce trends is vital for staying competitive in the labor market.

Remote Work: Embrace remote work and flexible work arrangements to recruit talent from a larger geographic region and suit the shifting preferences of the workforce.

Diversity and Inclusion: Promote diversity and inclusion to develop a more inventive and resilient workforce.

Technology Integration: Leverage technology to boost productivity, collaboration, and employee engagement.

Attracting and maintaining great talent is a constant process that demands a deliberate strategy and continued effort. By developing a compelling employer brand, adopting successful recruiting techniques, providing a happy work environment, and delivering chances for advancement and recognition, you can create a workplace that attracts and keeps the greatest personnel. This will be a crucial driver of your business's success as you expand from $1 million to $10 million and beyond.

CHAPTER 3

MARKETING AND SALES

Scaling Your Marketing Strategy

As your firm grows, scaling your marketing plan is critical to generating success. You may reach new audiences, build brand recognition, and produce leads that can become customers with the aid of a well-thought-out marketing plan. Understanding your market, creating a scalable marketing plan, using digital marketing, and tracking results are some of the essential elements of scaling your marketing strategy that will be covered in this chapter.

Gaining Knowledge of Your Market

It is essential to have a thorough grasp of your industry before developing your marketing strategy.

Market Research: Learn all you can about your target market's requirements, tastes, and habits by doing in-depth market research. Determine the prospects and market trends that may guide your marketing plan.

Customer Segmentation: Divide your consumer base into discrete categories according to psychographics, behavior, and demographics. This will enable you to more successfully target various groups with your marketing campaigns.

Competitive Analysis: Examine your rivals' strategy, advantages, and disadvantages. Determine the market gaps that you can fill and the places where your brand can stand out.

Formulating an Expandable Marketing Strategy

A scalable marketing strategy offers a path to accomplishing your expansion goals:

Define Objectives: Clearly state what you want to achieve with your marketing, e.g., raising sales, generating leads, or raising brand recognition. Make sure these goals are in line with your overarching company objectives.

Identify Key Metrics: Determine the key performance indicators, such as customer acquisition cost (CAC), lifetime value (LTV), and return on investment (ROI), you will use to assess the effectiveness of your marketing campaigns.

Money Allocation: Distribute your marketing money across various campaigns and channels in accordance with your goals and the anticipated return on investment. As you collect information and determine what works best, be ready to make adjustments to your budget allocation.

Making Use of Digital Marketing

Reaching your target audience may be accomplished in scalable and economical ways with digital marketing.

Material Marketing: To draw in and keep your target audience interested, create and disseminate useful, relevant material as part of a content marketing plan. Infographics, videos, whitepapers, and blog entries may all fall under this category.

Social Media Marketing: Promote your brand, engage with your audience, and exchange content via social media channels. Create a social media schedule to guarantee regular posting and interaction.

Email Marketing: Create and organize your

email list to send recipients customized, relevant content. Email marketing initiatives may be used to nurture prospects and turn them into paying clients.

Search Engine Optimization (SEO): To improve organic traffic, make sure your website and content are search engine optimized. To raise your search engine rankings, concentrate on both on-page and off-page SEO strategies.

Paid Advertising: To reach a wider audience and increase targeted traffic to your website, use paid advertising channels like Google Ads, Facebook Ads, and LinkedIn Ads. To maximize ROI, track and improve your advertising initiatives.

Reach Extension

To increase your reach, look into new markets and distribution methods.

Influencer Marketing: Collaborate with industry influencers to connect with their audience and establish your brand's legitimacy. Select influencers that really connect with their audience and whose beliefs match your business.

Collaborations and Alliances: Create strategic alliances and collaborations with other companies to broaden your clientele and get access to untapped markets. Seek out partners that share your target demographic and enhance your products.

International Expansion: To take advantage of fresh growth prospects, think about entering other markets. To comprehend the cultural, legal, and economic aspects that might affect your marketing plan in other locales, do market research.

Performance Measurement and Optimization

Ensuring the efficacy of your marketing endeavors requires measuring and improving performance.

Analytics and Reporting: Monitor the effectiveness of your marketing initiatives with the use of analytics tools. Keep an eye on important indicators like website traffic, conversion rates, and client acquisition expenses.

A/B Testing: Use A/B testing to compare and ascertain which iterations of your marketing materials work better. Utilize the knowledge gathered from these experiments to improve your advertising.

Continuous Improvement: Review and improve your marketing plan on a regular basis in response to feedback and performance data. Remain flexible and prepared to change course as necessary to meet your goals.

By expanding your marketing plan, you may draw in more clients, improve brand awareness, and promote long-term development. A solid marketing strategy, reinforced by digital marketing techniques and ongoing optimization, can assist you in accomplishing your objectives and setting up your company for long-term success.

Playbooks and Processes for Creating a Sales Machine

You need a well-oiled sales engine that can reliably turn leads into customers if you want to see sustained development. Creating strong sales playbooks, solid sales procedures, and ongoing approach optimization are all necessary to build a scalable sales engine. In this chapter, you will be guided through the essential elements of creating a scalable sales engine.

Creating Efficient Sales Procedures

Good sales procedures provide a methodical way to handle leads and close transactions.

Lead creation: Formulate an outward and inbound lead creation plan. Utilize social media, content marketing, and marketing campaigns to generate leads. To find possible clients, use cold-calling and email outreach strategies.

Lead qualifying: To find high-quality leads with a higher conversion rate, put in place a lead qualifying procedure. To evaluate leads, use BANT (budget, authority, need, and schedule) criteria.

Sales Funnel Management: Lay down the steps in your sales funnel, starting with the first contact and ending with deal closure. Clearly outline the steps and requirements needed to advance leads through each funnel level.

Customer Relationship Management (CRM): Manage leads, opportunities, and customer interactions using a CRM system. A CRM system helps make sure that no leads are overlooked by giving you insight into your sales funnel.

Making Playbooks for Sales

Your sales team may succeed by using sales playbooks to provide them with the resources and direction they require.

Standard Operating Procedures (SOPs): Create SOPs for important sales tasks, including qualifying leads, showcasing products, and drafting proposals. SOPs guarantee that your sales procedures are efficient and consistent.

Sales Scripts: Write scripts for the various phases of the sales process, such as the first outreach, the follow-up calls, and the closing discussions. Sales scripts facilitate efficient communication and objection handling among your team.

Objection Handling: Describe how to respond to typical objections that come up in the course of the sales process. Give your sales staff the tools they need to successfully handle objections and convert them into possibilities.

Case Studies and Testimonials: To highlight the benefits of your goods or services, use case studies and testimonials in your sales playbooks. Using real-world examples with prospective clients helps establish credibility and confidence.

Establishing a Sales Force That Performs Well

To spur development and meet your sales targets, you need a top-notch sales team.

Hiring the Right Talent: Look for salespeople

that possess the knowledge, expertise, and work ethic necessary to be successful in your company. Seek applicants who have shown results-oriented behavior, resilience, and motivation.

Training and Development: Make an investment in courses that will improve the abilities and expertise of your sales force. Ongoing instruction on product characteristics, sales strategies, and market developments should be given.

Performance Metrics: To gauge the effectiveness of your sales force, use key performance indicators (KPIs). Keep track of data like the sales cycle duration, average transaction size, and sales conversion rate.

Incentives and Rewards: To inspire your sales force, put incentive and reward systems into place. Provide commissions, incentives, and praise for exceeding sales goals and exhibiting superior performance.

Using Technology to Increase Sales

Technology may improve your sales machine's efficacy and efficiency.

Sales Automation: Automate repetitive operations like data input, appointment scheduling, and email follow-ups by using sales automation solutions. Your sales force can concentrate on high-value tasks thanks to automation.

Sales Enablement: Put sales enablement solutions into place to provide your team with the tools and data they need to close deals. This might include having access to training materials, customer data, and sales collateral.

Data Analytics: Make use of data analytics to learn more about your sales success and pinpoint areas that need work. Utilize data to anticipate sales, monitor trends, and enhance your sales approach.

Ongoing Enhancement and Streamlining

It needs constant development to keep up a high-performing sales machine.

Regular Reviews: Evaluate your playbooks, team performance, and sales procedures on a regular basis. Determine areas that need improvement and put new ideas into practice to increase productivity and effectiveness.

Feedback Loop: Create a channel of communication for feedback between your sales force and other divisions, such as product development and marketing. Utilize feedback to enhance your sales strategy and resolve any difficulties that may come up.

Adaptability: Remain flexible and prepared to modify your sales approach in response to shifts in the market, input from customers, and performance information. Maintaining the effectiveness and competitiveness of your sales machine is ensured by ongoing optimization.

You can reach your company objectives and produce continuous revenue growth by creating a scalable sales machine with reliable playbooks, strong procedures, and an exceptional staff. Utilizing technology and keeping an eye on ongoing development can help you keep your firm competitive and set it up for long-term success.

Using Technology in Marketing and Sales

When it comes to growing your marketing and sales operations, technology is essential. Using the appropriate tools and platforms can help you increase productivity, boost client engagement, and provide better outcomes. We'll look at how the use of technology can help your sales and marketing tactics in this chapter.

Automated Marketing

Tools for marketing automation that maximize and simplify your marketing activities include the following:

Automated Email Marketing: Segment your audience, customize messaging, and automate email campaigns using email marketing platforms. You can develop connections and nurture leads at scale using automation.

Social Media Management: Put social media into practice, Using management tools to plan posts, track interactions, and evaluate results across various media. You can keep up a steady social media presence by using automation.

Lead Scoring and Nurturing: Sort leads

according to their activities and interactions with your business by using marketing automation. Workflows for lead nurturing may be automated to provide relevant content and advance leads through the sales funnel.

CRM stands for Customer Relationship Management.

To manage client connections and sales operations, a CRM system is necessary.

Lead and Contact Management: Track interactions, handle follow-ups, and store and organize lead and contact data using CRM. A consolidated picture of your client data is offered by a CRM system.

Sales Pipeline Management: Use CRM to estimate sales, monitor prospects, and manage your sales pipeline. CRM guarantees that no leads are missed and assists you in keeping track of your sales efforts.

Customer Insights: Use CRM to learn about the preferences, behavior, and past purchases of your customers. Make use of this information to target your sales and marketing campaigns.

Business Intelligence and Data Analytics

Tools for business intelligence and data analytics provide insightful information about your marketing and sales success.

Performance Tracking: Monitor important performance indicators, such as website traffic, conversion rates, and sales income, using analytics tools. Keep an eye on these indicators to evaluate the success of your efforts.

Customer Segmentation: Use customer data analysis to divide up your audience into groups according to their preferences, behavior, and demographics. You may send marketing messages that are more relevant and focused by using segmentation.

Predictive Analytics: Make use of predictive analytics to pinpoint possible opportunities and project future sales patterns. Make use of predictive insights to guide your sales and marketing plans.

Management of the Customer Experience

Improving the client experience is essential for increasing retention and loyalty.

Consumer Feedback Tools: Gather and analyze consumer feedback with the help of these tools. Use evaluations, ratings, and surveys to learn about consumer satisfaction and pinpoint areas that need work.

Personalization: Make use of technology to tailor the client experience at various points of contact. Deliver individualized offers, suggestions, and content by using data.

Customer service: Use technologies like chatbots, live chat, and helpdesk software to deliver prompt and effective customer service. Boost client satisfaction overall and respond more quickly.

Technology to Enable Sales

Technology that facilitates sales gives your sales force the tools they need to close deals:

Content Management: Manage and distribute sales material, such as brochures, presentations, and case studies, using sales enablement tools. Make sure the material your sales staff has access to is current and relevant.

Training and Coaching: Give your sales force continual education and assistance by putting in place coaching and training resources. To improve abilities and knowledge, make use of performance monitoring, video coaching, and e-learning platforms.

Sales Analytics: Monitor sales results, spot patterns, and enhance your approach to selling by using sales analytics tools. To enhance sales procedures and provide better outcomes, use data-driven insights.

Combining Marketing and Sales Technologies

Data exchange and cooperation are certain to run well when your sales and marketing tools are integrated.

CRM and Marketing Integration: To guarantee seamless lead and customer data transfer across systems, integrate your CRM system with your marketing automation platform. Improved lead monitoring and management are made possible by this connection.

Data Synchronization: To provide a cohesive picture of client interactions, make sure your marketing and sales technology are in sync. Data synchronization enhances decision-making and aids in the removal of silos.

Workflow Automation: To increase efficiency and simplify procedures, use workflow automation. Automate processes like data input, follow-up reminders, and lead handoff.

Up-and-Coming Technologies

Examine and take up new technology to stay ahead of the curve.

Artificial Intelligence (AI): Use AI to improve your marketing and sales initiatives. Make use of chatbots, lead scoring, tailored suggestions, and predictive analytics driven by AI.

Machine Learning (ML): Use ML to examine huge datasets and find trends that might help guide your tactics. Utilize machine learning (ML) to boost client segmentation, targeting, and campaign optimization.

Blockchain: Learn about blockchain technology for safe and open transactions, particularly in sectors where data integrity and trust are vital. Blockchain is also useful for safe data sharing and loyalty schemes.

Optimal Methods for Utilizing Technology

Utilize these recommended practices to get the most out of technology:

Select the Right Tools: Make technological decisions in line with the objectives and demands of your company. Consider your alternatives and choose tools with the features and functionalities you need.

Implementation and Training: Make sure your team members get the necessary training and that you have a well-thought-out implementation strategy. To get the most out of your technological expenditures, proper implementation and training are crucial.

Continuous Evaluation: Assess your technological solutions' performance on a regular basis and make necessary improvements. To be sure you are using the newest features and capabilities, keep up with upgrades and new innovations.

Data Security: When putting technological solutions into practice, give data security and privacy first priority. Make sure your tools adhere to applicable laws and have safeguards in place to secure client information.

You may improve sales and marketing efforts, get better results, and set up your company for expansion by using technology wisely. Accept the digital age and maintain your flexibility to adjust to shifting consumer demands and market circumstances. Your success when you grow your company from $1 million to $10 million and beyond will be greatly aided by technology.

CHAPTER 4

OPERATIONS AND EFFICIENCY

Streamlining Operations for Scalability

For a firm to go from $1 million to $10 million, operational simplification must be a strategic priority. Scalable growth relies on efficient processes, which allow your company to develop without sacrificing quality or customer happiness. The main tactics for optimizing your processes to guarantee scalability will be covered in this chapter. These tactics include improving supply chain management, using technology, and simplifying processes.

Evaluating Current Activities

You must comprehend your existing operating environment before you can streamline operations.

Operational examine: To find inefficiencies and bottlenecks, thoroughly examine your present operations. Examine every step of the process, from delivery to manufacturing to procurement, and determine how successful it is.

Employee Feedback: To learn more about operational difficulties and possible enhancements, collect input from staff members across all levels. Frontline staff members often provide insightful viewpoints on routine procedures.

Customer Feedback: Get input from clients to learn about their experiences and pinpoint any areas where your business could be lacking. Make your improvement priorities based on this input to increase customer happiness.

Optimization of Processes

Achieving operational efficiency requires process optimization.

Mapping Processes: To see every stage of your processes, make thorough process maps. This makes it easier to see delays, redundant information, and areas where you can streamline.

Standardization: To guarantee efficiency and uniformity, standardize procedures. Create best practices outlined in standard operating procedures (SOPs) and make sure that every employee abides by them.

Automation: To cut down on manual labor and boost productivity, automate wherever feasible. Numerous procedures, including order processing, inventory management, and customer support, may be automated.

Lean Principles: Use lean concepts to cut waste and enhance workflow. Reducing non-value-added tasks and maximizing resource utilization should be your main priorities.

Continuous Improvement: Create a culture in which staff members are motivated to find and recommend ways to improve processes. Review and improve procedures often to accommodate changing requirements and circumstances.

Making Use of Technology

Technology is essential for facilitating scalability and simplifying operations.

Enterprise Resource Planning (ERP): Set up an ERP system to coordinate and oversee key corporate operations, including supply chain, finance, HR, and procurement. Real-time visibility and control over your activities are made possible with an ERP system.

Inventory Management Systems: To maximize stock levels, save carrying costs, and avoid stockouts, use inventory management systems. To guarantee inventory correctness, use automatic reordering and real-time tracking.

Customer Relationship Management (CRM): A CRM system facilitates better customer service, sales tracking, and customer interaction management. To improve the customer experience and expedite information flow, integrate CRM with other platforms.

Project Management Tools: To successfully plan, carry out, and oversee projects, use project management tools. These technologies make it easier to work together, monitor development, and guarantee that projects are completed on time and under budget.

Data Analytics: Use data analytics to uncover

areas that need improvement and to get insights into operational performance. Utilize analytics to streamline procedures and create data-driven choices.

Improving Management of the Supply Chain

Scalable operations need the backing of a strong supply chain.

Supplier Relationships: Establish solid bonds with dependable suppliers to guarantee goods are delivered on schedule and with consistent quality. Create cooperative alliances and open lines of communication.

supplier Chain Visibility: Put in place tools that provide you instant access to information about your supplier chain. Keep an eye on inventory levels, follow the flow of items, and look out for any possible disturbances.

Demand Forecasting: Project future demand

using demand forecasting methodologies, then adjust your supply chain appropriately. Precise prediction aids in cutting surplus inventories and avoiding stockouts.

Logistics Optimization: To increase the efficacy and economy of your distribution and transportation operations, optimize your logistics. When necessary, make use of third-party logistics providers, load optimization, and route planning.

Risk Management: To identify and reduce supply chain risks, create a risk management plan. Establish backup plans in case of unforeseen circumstances, such as delayed or non-functioning suppliers.

Expanding Employee Activities

One essential element of scalable operations is your workforce.

Workforce Planning: Create a workforce strategy that complements your goals for development. Determine the roles and competencies required to support your operations as you grow.

Training and Development: Make an investment in training and development initiatives to provide your staff members with the abilities and know-how necessary for smooth operations. Sustaining high performance is facilitated by ongoing learning and growth.

Employee Engagement: Promote an atmosphere at work that is conducive to the engagement and productivity of employees. Employee contributions should be acknowledged and rewarded, and development opportunities should be offered.

Labor Efficiency: Increase labor efficiency via the use of technology to assist workforce management, flexible work arrangements, and staff cross-training.

Operational Performance Measuring

Measurement of operational performance is necessary to make sure your streamlining initiatives are successful.

Key Performance Indicators (KPIs): Determine and monitor KPIs that demonstrate the effectiveness and efficiency of your operations. Cycle time, defect rates, order fulfillment time, and customer satisfaction are examples of common KPIs.

Benchmarking: To find areas for improvement, assess your performance in relation to industry benchmarks. By benchmarking your operations, you may see how they compare to those of your rivals and industry best practices.

Performance evaluations: Evaluate progress

made toward operational objectives by conducting frequent performance evaluations. Utilize these evaluations to pinpoint achievements, deal with difficulties, and make plans for ongoing development.

Your operations may be streamlined to lay the groundwork for scalable expansion. Enhanced supply chain management, a trained staff, technological leverage, and process optimization can help your company meet growth goals and manage rising demand.

Putting in Place Effective Procedures and Systems

Effective system and process implementation is essential for company growth. Efficiency raises customer happiness, productivity, and quality while lowering expenses. The implementation of effective systems and processes will be examined in this chapter, along with methods for system integration, process automation, and continuous improvement.

Integration of Systems

Integrating systems across your company guarantees efficient operations and smooth information flow.

Data Integration: To link dissimilar systems and guarantee that data is shared across the company, use data integration solutions. A single source of truth is offered by integrated data, which also facilitates well-informed decision-making.

Unified Platforms: To centralize processes and cut complexity, use unified platforms, such as ERP systems, that incorporate numerous tasks. Workflows are streamlined, and cooperation is enhanced via unified platforms.

API Integration: Connect various software programs by using API (Application Programming Interface) integration. Real-time data interchange and system interoperability are made possible via APIs.

Cloud Solutions: To improve scalability, accessibility, and flexibility, use cloud-based solutions. System integration, data storage, and remote work are all supported by cloud solutions.

Automation of Processes

Process automation may greatly increase productivity and lower mistake rates.

Robotic Process Automation (RPA): Use RPA to automate rule-based, repetitive operations like order management, data input, and invoice processing. RPA improves accuracy while releasing staff to work on higher-value tasks.

Workflow Automation: To assure consistent execution of complicated procedures, use workflow automation solutions. Task assignments, alerts, and approvals are all managed with the use of workflow automation.

company Process Management (BPM): Use BPM to plan, organize, carry out, keep an eye on, and improve company processes. BPM technologies provide a methodical way to raise the efficacy and efficiency of processes.

Intelligent Automation: To automate more complicated activities and make wise judgments, combine RPA with machine learning (ML) and artificial intelligence (AI). Capabilities are improved, and creativity is stimulated by intelligent automation.

Improving Interaction and Teamwork

Streamlined operations need effective teamwork and communication.

Collaboration platforms: To promote communication and cooperation, make use of collaboration platforms like Asana, Microsoft Teams, and Slack. Project management, file sharing, and real-time communications are supported by these programs.

Video Conferencing: Use video conferencing tools to facilitate online collaboration and distant meetings. Teams that are geographically separated may stay connected and engaged by using video conferencing.

Document Management: To safely organize, store, and distribute documents, use document management solutions. Systems for managing documents improve version control and accessibility.

Knowledge Sharing: Encourage a culture of

knowledge sharing among staff members by setting up sites, such as wikis and intranets, where they may exchange data, best practices, and resources.

Ongoing Improvement

Sustaining productivity and fostering long-term success need constant improvement.

Lean and Six Sigma: Use these techniques to find and remove waste, cut down on variability, and enhance process quality. These techniques provide a methodical way to approach ongoing development.

Kaizen: Put into practice the Kaizen concept, which emphasizes frequent small-scale improvements produced by all staff members. Kaizen promotes creativity and proactive approaches to problem-solving.

Performance Monitoring: Use KPIs and other

measures to continuously track performance. Review performance data on a regular basis to find areas that need improvement and put remedial measures in place.

Employee Involvement: Encourage staff members to provide ideas and take part in improvement projects in order to include them in ongoing efforts for continuous improvement. Employee participation promotes an accountable and ownership culture.

Handling Transition

To effectively integrate new systems and procedures, effective change management is necessary.

Change Management Strategy: Create a thorough strategy, including the resources, timetable, and actions needed to accomplish the changes. A clear strategy facilitates a seamless transition management process.

Communication Strategy: Explain to all parties involved the goals and advantages of the change. To make sure that everyone receives the message and that any issues are addressed, use a variety of channels.

Training and assistance: Assist staff members in adjusting to new procedures and systems by offering them assistance and training. To guarantee a seamless transfer, provide seminars, hands-on training, and continuing assistance.

Feedback Mechanism: Create a feedback system to get staff feedback while the implementation is underway. Utilize these suggestions to make changes and resolve any problems in a timely manner.

Best Practices and Case Studies

Gaining knowledge from effective case studies

and best practices may help develop effective systems and procedures.

Case Study Analysis: Examine case studies of businesses that have effectively incorporated effective procedures and systems. Determine the tactics and methods that helped them succeed.

Industry Best Practices: Find and implement industry best practices that complement your operations and commercial objectives. Proven techniques for attaining scalability and efficiency are found in best practices.

Benchmarking: Evaluate your procedures in comparison to industry norms and top businesses. To find weaknesses and potential development areas, use benchmarking.

You can promote scalable growth, save expenses, and increase productivity by putting in place effective systems and procedures. Creating a streamlined and productive organization requires a strong foundation in integration, automation, continuous improvement, and effective change management.

Financial Planning and Cash Flow Management

Financial planning and efficient cash flow management are essential to the expansion and long-term viability of your company. Maintaining a solid cash flow and putting strong financial planning procedures in place can guarantee that you have the resources required to support your development as you expand from $1 million to $10 million. The methods for controlling cash flow, financial planning, forecasting, and budgeting will all be covered in this chapter.

Getting to Know Cash Flow

It is crucial to comprehend cash flow in order to preserve financial stability.

Fundamentals of Cash Flow: The flow of funds into and out of your company is referred to as cash flow. When inflows are greater than outflows, there is positive cash flow; when the opposite is true, there is negative cash flow.

Cash Flow Statement: This financial statement includes all of the cash inflows and outflows for a certain time period. It offers information on funding, investing, and operational operations.

Cash Flow Management

Having good cash flow management guarantees that your company has the liquidity it needs to run and expand.

Cash Flow Forecasting: To predict future cash inflows and outflows, create a cash flow forecast. To produce a reliable prediction, use sales estimations, historical data, and spending estimates.

Accounts Receivable Management: Put measures into place to efficiently handle accounts receivable. Provide rewards for early payments, lay out precise conditions for payments, and immediately pursue past-due bills.

Inventory Management: To save expenses and free up cash, optimize inventory levels. To precisely monitor stock levels, employ inventory management systems and just-in-time inventory techniques.

Expense Control: Keep an eye on and rein on spending to keep cash flow positive. Determine where expenses may be cut without sacrificing product or service quality.

Financing alternatives: To meet your short-term cash flow demands, look into financing alternatives, including factoring, loans, and credit lines. Make sure you comprehend the conditions and expenses related to each choice.

Financial Planning and Budgeting

Sophisticated financial planning and budgeting are necessary to meet your development goals.

Annual Budgeting: Create a yearly budget that details your anticipated income, outlays, and cash flows. Make financial choices about your spending and investments by using the budget as a guide.

Variance Analysis: Use variance analysis to see how the budgeted amount and actual financial performance differ. Determine the causes of deviations and make the necessary adjustments to remain on course.

Scenario Planning: Make plans for various financial situations by using scenario planning. Create worst-case, best-case, and most probable scenarios to see how they could affect your cash flow and financial standing.

Capital Expenditure Planning: Make plans for capital expenditures (CAPEX) that will help businesses grow, such as new technology, expanded facilities, and equipment acquisitions. Make sure you have the money or the financing needed to pay for these investments.

Accounting Prediction

You may predict future financial performance and make wise choices by using financial forecasting.

Sales Forecasting: Create sales projections by analyzing the sales pipeline, market trends, and historical data. Planning for inventory, personnel, and cash flow requirements is facilitated by accurate sales forecasting.

Expense Forecasting: Project costs by looking at past trends in expenditure and projecting future requirements. Add both fixed and variable expenses, and take demand and price fluctuations into consideration.

Cash Flow Projections: To predict future cash inflows and outflows, create cash flow projections. Make plans for financial requirements and spot any cash shortfalls by using these forecasts.

Profit and Loss Forecasting: To anticipate future revenues, costs, and profits, create profit and loss (P&L) forecasts. You may assess the financial sustainability of your expansion initiatives with the use of P&L predictions.

Risk Management in Finance

Sustaining financial stability requires effective risk management.

Risk Assessment: Recognize possible financial hazards, including fluctuations in interest rates, market volatility, and economic downturns. Evaluate each risk's probability and potential effects on your company.

Risk Mitigation: Reduce the effect of financial risks by putting risk mitigation techniques into practice. Manage currency and interest rate risks by using hedging mechanisms, keeping cash reserves, and diversifying your income sources.

Insurance: Get insurance to guard against monetary losses resulting from unanticipated circumstances, including property damage, liability lawsuits, and company disruption. Make sure your insurance is current and sufficient.

Analysis and Reporting on Finance

Frequent financial reporting and analysis shed light on the financial well-being of your company.

Financial Statements: Compile and examine the cash flow, income, and balance sheets, among other important financial statements. These statements provide you with a thorough understanding of your performance and financial situation.

Key Financial Statistics: Examine important financial statistics to determine the state of your company's finances, including leverage, profitability, and liquidity ratios. To determine your strengths and potential development areas, use these ratios.

Benchmarking: Assess your competitiveness by comparing your financial performance to industry benchmarks. You may find best practices and make realistic financial objectives with the aid of benchmarking.

Financial Dashboards: To see important financial indicators and trends, use financial dashboards. Dashboards let you make data-driven choices by giving you real-time information.

Financial Strategy and Planning

Your financial aims and company goals are in line when you use strategic financial planning.

Long-Term Financial Goals: Establish long-term financial objectives, including revenue targets, profit margins, and return on investment (ROI), that are consistent with your growth vision. Make sure these objectives are doable and reasonable.

Investment Strategy: Create a plan for your investments that strikes a balance between return and risk. Invest resources in high-impact initiatives that boost competitiveness and promote growth.

Exit Strategy: Make plans for possible exit tactics, including acquisitions, mergers, and initial public offers (IPOs). Think about the financial ramifications and have your company ready for a smooth departure if necessary.

Financial Technology Utilization

Your ability to handle your finances may be improved by financial technology, or FinTech.

Accounting Software: To automate financial transactions, monitor spending, and provide financial reports, use accounting software. Accounting software lessens administrative work and increases accuracy.

cost management solutions: To expedite the procedures of cost reporting, approval, and reimbursement, use expense management solutions. These tools improve expenditure visibility and management.

Cash Flow Management Applications: These applications let you automate payments and invoices, predict future cash demands, and keep an eye on your cash flow in real time. These applications enhance cash flow planning and help preserve liquidity.

Financial Analytics Platforms: Examine financial data, spot patterns, and provide insights by using financial analytics platforms. These platforms facilitate strategic planning and data-driven decision-making.

Through efficient cash flow management and the

use of sound financial planning techniques, you can guarantee that your company has the resources required to facilitate scalable expansion. Staying financially stable and reaching your development goals requires an understanding of cash flow, budgeting, forecasting, risk management, and using FinTech.

CHAPTER 5

GROWTH AND EXPANSION

Identifying New Markets and Opportunities

Taking advantage of opportunities and venturing into new areas are essential to growing your company from $1 million to $10 million. It takes careful preparation, extensive study, and strategic analysis to recognize and seize these chances. This chapter will examine methods for locating untapped markets and business possibilities, evaluating their feasibility, and developing entry and exit plans.

Analysis and Research on the Market

Finding new prospects requires doing thorough market research and analysis.

Market Segmentation: Using psychographics, behavior, location, and demographics, divide the large market into smaller, easier-to-manage groups. Knowing the various market groups enables you to customize your strategy and spot opportunities in specialized markets.

Competitive Analysis: To comprehend the environment, carry out a comprehensive competitive analysis. Determine your competitors—both direct and indirect—and evaluate their positions in the market, as well as their advantages and disadvantages. This aids in identifying holes and chances for differentiation.

Customer Insights: Conduct focus groups, interviews, and surveys to get direct feedback from prospective consumers. Unmet demands and new market prospects may be found by understanding their preferences, wants, and pain areas.

Industry Trends: Keep up with developments in technology, legislation, and industry trends. Trends may help you remain ahead of the competition by indicating new possibilities.

SWOT Analysis: Evaluate your company's internal and external environments by conducting a SWOT analysis (Strengths, Weaknesses, Opportunities, Threats). This all-encompassing perspective aids in locating and ranking fresh chances.

Determining the Marketability

Every market is not made equal. Evaluating a new market's feasibility is essential.

Market Size and Growth: Assess the market's size and room for expansion. Greater prospects for expansion and profitability are presented by large and expanding markets.

Market Demand: Determine if there is a need

in the new market for your goods or services. Keep an eye out for signs like the presence of rivals, consumer interest, and market preparedness.

Entrance Barriers: Determine possible obstacles to entrance, such as legal specifications, cultural disparities, and the level of competition. Comprehending these obstacles facilitates risk mitigation and planning.

Examine the market's possible profitability. Take into account variables like margin expectations, cost structures, and pricing power.

Strategic Fit: Verify that the new market complements the advantages and long-term objectives of your company. Your chances of success rise when you enter a market where you can exploit your core talents.

Formulating Strategies for Entering Markets

Upon identification of a feasible market, it is essential to devise a comprehensive entrance plan.

Market Penetration: This tactic entails bringing current items into a new market. Concentrate on expanding your market share through aggressive marketing, competitive pricing, and first-rate customer support.

Market Development: Adapt your current offerings to suit the demands of expanding markets or new target audiences. This might include new packaging, modified products, or adjustments to marketing tactics.

Product Development: Launch new items that cater to the particular requirements of the expanding market. This may require a great deal of R&D and in-depth knowledge of the tastes of the local market.

Diversification: Launch new goods into an

entirely untapped market. A significant financial commitment and in-depth knowledge of the market are necessary for this high-risk, high-reward approach.

Allies and Partnerships: To ease market access, work with regional distributors, agents, or companies. Reduced entrance hurdles, existing client bases, and local market expertise are some benefits of partnerships.

Approach to the Market

A successful market launch is guaranteed by a well-thought-out go-to-market (GTM) strategy:

Market Positioning: Make sure your brand is well understood in the new market. Your placement has to set you apart from rivals and appeal to local customers.

Promotion and Marketing: Create a marketing strategy specific to the new market. To increase brand recognition, combine conventional advertising, public relations, internet marketing, and local events.

Sales Strategy: Specify your sales approach, including the structure of your sales team, sales methods, and sales channels (direct, indirect, online, and offline). Educate and equip your sales force to handle the demands of the expanding market.

Pricing Strategy: Determine prices in accordance with the competitive environment, consumer expectations, and market circumstances. Think about approaches such as value-based pricing, premium pricing, or penetration pricing.

Distribution and Logistics: Arrange your logistics and distribution to guarantee timely delivery and product availability. Think about regional alliances, storage options, and the logistics of transit.

Observing and Modifying

Entering a new market is a continuing process that involves regular monitoring and adjustments.

Performance Metrics: To monitor your advancement, set up key performance indicators (KPIs). Market share, revenue growth, customer acquisition expenses, and profitability are examples of common KPIs.

Feedback Loops: Put in place systems to get input from partners, clients, and staff. Make the required changes to your strategy and operations based on this input.

Market Dynamics: Be mindful of any changes to the market's dynamics, including the entry of new rivals, alterations to laws or regulations, or adjustments in consumer preferences. Be ready to change courses as necessary.

Continuous Improvement: Evaluate and improve your market entry plan on a regular basis. Maintaining your competitiveness and adaptability to market changes is ensured by continuous development.

Your company may effectively enter new markets and take advantage of growth possibilities by carefully investigating and evaluating them, determining their feasibility, and creating a clear entry strategy.

Cooperative and Strategic Alliances

Collaborations and strategic alliances may be effective engines for corporate development. Through the use of other businesses' strengths and talents, you may expand into new areas, improve your products and services, and create successful synergies. The advantages of strategic partnerships, their formation and identification, and the upkeep and management of these connections for sustained success are all covered in this chapter.

Advantages of Strategic Alliances

The numerous advantages of strategic alliances might hasten development.

Market Access: Partners may provide entry to untapped consumer groups, distribution networks, and marketplaces. This is particularly helpful when joining new or foreign markets.

Resource Sharing: Through partnerships, you may pool resources like infrastructure, knowledge, and technology to save expenses and boost productivity.

Risk Mitigation: By splitting the financial load and lowering exposure to market uncertainty, working with partners may help reduce risks.

Innovation: New product development and innovation are fostered by partners' complementary abilities and new insights.

Competitive Advantage: By merging strengths and developing distinctive value propositions, strategic alliances may improve your competitive position.

Finding Possible Allies

Selecting the appropriate partners is essential to a successful collaboration.

Alignment of Goals: Seek companions who share your beliefs and aspirations. A successful collaboration requires that both parties have the same goal and vision.

Complementary qualities: Find partners whose skills and qualities complement one another. For instance, having a partner with good distribution skills might be advantageous if you are an excellent product developer.

Reputation and Reliability: Evaluate possible partners' credibility and dependability. To be sure they have a successful and honest history, do your research.

Cultural Fit: In foreign relationships in particular, cultural fit is crucial. Make sure that everyone respects and is aware of one another's corporate cultures.

Strategic Fit: Consider how the alliance fits with your overarching business strategy. Your competitive advantage and long-term development should both benefit from this cooperation.

Forming Strategic Alliances

Careful preparation and unambiguous agreements are essential to creating a successful partnership.

Define Objectives: Clearly state what the collaboration hopes to accomplish. What are your goals, and how will you determine if you've succeeded?

Partnership Structure: Choose how the partnership will be organized. Is it going to be a contractual partnership, a joint venture, or a strategic alliance? The degree of integration and dedication should be reflected in the structure.

Roles and Responsibilities: Clearly state what each partner's obligations are. Specify who will be in charge of certain duties, decision-making procedures, and responsibility areas.

Legal Agreements: Create thorough legal agreements that address every facet of the collaboration, such as confidentiality, intellectual property rights, conditions of participation, and exit plans. Seek legal advice to make sure all the details are taken care of.

Communication strategy: To guarantee consistent and open communication between partners, create a communication strategy. This covers gatherings, channels for reporting, and procedures for resolving disputes.

Handling and Developing Collaborations

Partnerships that succeed need constant upkeep and care.

Regular Review Meetings: Arrange frequent gatherings to discuss obstacles, assess advancements, and make required modifications. Keeping lines of communication open facilitates problem solutions.

Performance measures: To gauge the partnership's success, set up and monitor performance measures. Assess performance against these measures on a regular basis to find areas that need work.

Collaboration and Trust: Establish consistent, just practices to foster trust. Encourage a culture of cooperation where partners are respected and feel appreciated.

Adaptability and Flexibility: Be ready to change courses as necessary. Roles, responsibilities, and tactics that are flexible may help overcome obstacles and take advantage of new possibilities.

Conflict Resolution: Create procedures for settling disputes swiftly and peacefully. Deal with problems as they come up to keep them from becoming worse and hurting the relationship.

Best Practices and Case Studies

Gaining knowledge from successful collaborations may provide insightful information.

Case Study Analysis: Examine examples of successful strategic alliances in your sector. List the main ingredients for success, the difficulties encountered, and the solutions found.

Optimal Techniques: Take after successful partnerships' best practices. Clear goal-setting, robust governance frameworks, good communication, and respect for one another are a few examples.

Industry Benchmarks: Evaluate your collaborations by comparing them to industry norms. To find weaknesses and potential development areas, use benchmarking.

Forming strategic alliances and working together may greatly accelerate the development trajectory of your company. By picking mates with care, making explicit commitments, and fostering the partnership, you may create synergies that promote efficiency, creativity, and market growth.

Acquisitions and Mergers: Growth Strategies

M&A, or mergers and acquisitions, are effective tactics for achieving quick development and expansion. Businesses may acquire new technology, expand their skills, enter new markets, and realize economies of scale via M&A. M&A does, however, also come with a lot of complexity and danger. The strategic factors, procedures, and best practices for mergers and acquisitions that lead to success will be examined in this chapter.

Strategic Aspects to Take into Account in M&A

Prior to considering M&A, strategic goals and fit must be taken into account.

Growth Objectives: Make sure you specify your goals for growth and how M&A will contribute to achieving them. Achieving cost savings, gaining technology, diversifying the business, and expanding the market are some examples of objectives.

Strategic Fit: Evaluate if possible targets are strategically fit. Think about things like your company's position in the market, your product line, your clientele, and cultural fit.

Value Creation: Determine the value that the purchase will add. Determine the synergies that will create value after the purchase, such as cost reductions, revenue increases, and capacity creation.

Financial Health: Evaluate the target company's financial situation. To comprehend their debt levels, cash flow, and profitability, do in-depth financial research.

Determining M&A Objectives

Researching potential M&A targets thoroughly and with a strategic focus is essential.

Market Analysis: Examine the market to find possible targets. Seek out businesses that have complementary qualities and are in line with your strategic aims.

Industry Networks: To find possible targets, make use of advisers, consultants, and industry networks. Networking may provide insightful information and beneficial chances.

Screening Criteria: Create a set of standards to assess possible candidates. Financial success, market position, strategic fit, and cultural compatibility are a few examples of such criteria.

Due Diligence: Perform thorough due diligence to evaluate the target's operational capabilities, legal status, financial stability, and cultural fit. Identifying risks and confirming the strategic justification need due diligence.

Process of M&A

There are several phases in the M&A process, ranging from integration to planning:

Planning and Strategy: Create a well-defined M&A plan that details your goals, target demographic, and methodology. Form an M&A team to supervise the process.

Valuation and Negotiation: Evaluate the target firm in great detail. Make use of a variety of valuation techniques, including prior transactions, similar business research, and discounted cash flow (DCF). Aim for advantageous conditions that support your strategic objectives.

Due Diligence: To identify any hidden risks or obligations, do thorough due diligence. The financial, legal, operational, and cultural aspects are all covered by due diligence.

Transaction Execution: Complete the deal by obtaining regulatory clearances and formal contracts. Make sure every phrase is spelled out in detail and approved in writing.

Integration Planning: Create an integration strategy that combines the two firms' systems, cultures, and operations. In order to guarantee a seamless transition, integration planning has to begin early.

Integration Following Merger

Achieving successful integration is essential to reaping M&A advantages.

Integration Teams: Form teams to supervise the integration process. These teams, which should include important areas like operations, finance, HR, and IT, should include people from both businesses.

Cultural Integration: Work to create a cohesive corporate culture by addressing cultural disparities. Effective cultural integration requires open communication and employee participation.

Operational Synergies: Find and use synergies that may boost income, save costs, or streamline processes. Monitor development and assess the synergy's effects.

Communication strategy: Create a strategy for informing all parties involved. Building trust and controlling expectations are facilitated by open and frequent communication.

Monitoring and Evaluation: Track the development of the integration process. Utilize performance metrics to evaluate the integration's effectiveness and make the required modifications.

M&A Risk Management

Significant risks associated with M&A must be properly addressed.

Financial Risks: Evaluate and control financial risks, including effects on cash flow, debt levels, and overvaluation. Do a complete stress test and financial analysis.

Operational Risks: Recognize potential operational hazards, including imperfect supply chains, difficult integrations, and incompatibility with IT systems. Create strategies for risk mitigation to handle these issues.

Risks Related to Law and Regulation: Make sure that all legal and regulatory obligations are met. Seek legal advice while navigating intricate regulatory environments.

Cultural hazards: Promote an inclusive and cooperative atmosphere to mitigate cultural hazards. Operational inefficiency and employee alienation may result from cultural mismatches.

Best Practices and Case Studies

Gaining important insights from successful M&A transactions may be achieved by:

Case Study Analysis: Examine case studies of M&A transactions that were successful and failed. List the most important success elements, typical hazards, and lessons learned.

Best Practices: Take note of what successful M&A transactions have done. These might include good risk management, transparent communication, robust integration planning, and careful due diligence.

Benchmarking: Compare your merger and acquisition procedures to industry norms. To strengthen your M&A strategy and pinpoint areas for improvement, use benchmarking.

Acquisitions and mergers are effective strategies for achieving quick development and growth. Through strategic goal-setting, target selection, and efficient M&A process management, your company may use M&A to gain a substantial competitive advantage and considerable value. To fully reap the rewards of mergers and acquisitions, effective risk management and post-merger integration are essential.

CHAPTER 6

OVERCOMING OBSTACLES

Handling Scaling Difficulties and Growth Pains

Growing a company from $1 million to $10 million is a difficult and demanding undertaking. Growth presents many opportunities, but it also poses serious obstacles and potential dangers. This chapter will examine typical scaling problems and growth pains and offer solutions for efficiently handling and resolving these issues.

Grasping the Idea of Growth Pains

The inevitable difficulties that come with expanding a business are known as growth pains. Operations, finance, human resources, and customer relations are just a few of the domains where these difficulties may appear.

Operational Strain: Existing operational systems and processes may be severely strained by rapid development. Demand growth could result in inefficiencies, bottlenecks, and problems with quality control.

Financial Stress: Significant financial resources are needed for scaling. It can get harder to maintain profitability, secure capital, and manage cash flow.

Human Resources Challenges: As a firm expands, finding, developing, and keeping talent is harder. Careful consideration must be given to organizational structure, employee involvement, and corporate culture.

Customer Service: As the clientele grows, it may be harder to maintain excellent standards of customer care. Managing client expectations and ensuring constant service quality are essential.

Leadership Strain: Times of fast expansion place a great deal of pressure on leadership. In addition to managing growing tasks, leaders also need to make strategic choices and deal with unpredictability.

Typical Scaling Errors

Scaling pitfalls are the particular errors and blunders that companies frequently make as they expand. It is possible to avoid these traps by being aware of them.

Overexpansion: Without enough planning, expanding too rapidly can result in resource depletion and operational turmoil. It's critical to strike a balance between expansion and management capabilities.

Underestimating Market Demand: Excess inventory or stock outs may arise from an incorrect assessment of market demand. Inventory control and precise demand predictions are essential.

Ignoring Scalability of Systems: It's possible that current procedures and systems aren't scalable. It is essential to invest in scalable infrastructure, such as reliable IT systems and automated procedures.

Losing Focus on Core Competencies: Diluting focus and resources might result from diversifying too quickly or pursuing unrelated company activities. Sustainable growth is guaranteed when fundamental competencies are maintained.

Inadequate Financial Planning: Cash flow problems and unstable finances can result from poor financial planning and mismanagement. Budgeting and detailed financial estimates are crucial.

Neglecting Customer Relationships: Customer relationships may be strained by rapid expansion. Putting the needs and loyalty of your customers first is essential for long-term success.

Cultural Dilution: A company's culture may be diluted by rapid growth. Employee engagement and retention depend on the organization's culture being preserved and strengthened.

Techniques for Handling Developmental Pain

Proactive measures and ongoing development are needed to handle growth pains effectively.

Scalable Operations: Spend money on procedures and operations that are scalable. To effectively handle rising demand, automate monotonous processes, optimize workflows, and put in place reliable IT systems.

Financial Management: Create thorough financial planning and uphold stringent spending guidelines. Maintain strict cash flow oversight, obtain the capital you need, and make sure your business is profitable by managing your finances wisely.

Human Resources Management: Assist with hiring, training, and employee relations by assembling a capable HR team. Put your attention on cultivating a supportive workplace environment and high staff morale.

Excellent Customer Service: Give top priority to customer service by making investments in systems for customer assistance, providing staff with training, and keeping channels of contact open with clients.

Leadership Development: Through mentoring and training, hone your leadership skills. Promote adaptability, strategic thinking, and decision-making in leadership teams.

Data-Driven Decision Making: Make decisions

by using analytics and data. Monitor key performance indicators (KPIs) and make use of the insights gained to streamline processes and tactics.

Risk Management: Determine possible hazards and create strategies to reduce them. Review and update risk management plans often to handle emerging issues.

Best Practices and Case Studies

Gaining knowledge from other companies' experiences might help you manage growing pains and steer clear of dangers.

Case Study Analysis: Examine case studies of businesses that have expanded successfully. Determine the tactics they employed to overcome obstacles and grow through growing pains.

Best Practices: Use best practices from the

industry to scale operations, finance, HR, and customer service. Compare your company's performance against that of successful ones to find areas that need work.

Continuous Learning: Promote ongoing development and learning inside the company. Keep yourself updated on evolving best practices, technology developments, and industry trends.

Businesses can create plans to successfully handle development pains and possible hazards by knowing and anticipating them. Successful scaling requires proactive planning, scalable operations, sound financial management, and a strong emphasis on culture and customer service.

Preserving Culture and Principles in the Face of Fast Development

Maintaining the fundamental culture and principles that have contributed to a business's success becomes more difficult when it grows quickly. Long-term sustainability, customer satisfaction, and employee engagement all depend on the culture and values of the organization. The methods for protecting and fostering culture and values in times of rapid development will be discussed in this chapter.

Organizational Culture Is Vital

The shared values, attitudes, and practices that characterize an organization's culture determine how its members interact and collaborate. A robust culture encourages:

Employee Engagement: Motivated, dedicated, and productive workers are those who are engaged. Positive workplace cultures lower turnover and increase job satisfaction.

Customer Satisfaction: Prioritizing the needs and expectations of customers results in increased satisfaction and loyalty when a company adopts a customer-centric culture.

Innovation and Creativity: Continuous improvement and flexibility are fostered by a culture that values innovation and creativity.

Brand Identity: The company's reputation and brand identity are strengthened by a strong internal and external culture.

Difficulties in Preserving Culture During Expansion

Several obstacles arise in the way of preserving a unified culture with rapid growth:

Geographic Dispersion: Communication obstacles and cultural differences may arise from expansion into new areas. It can be difficult to maintain a uniform culture across several locations.

Increased Workforce: A quickly expanding workforce has the potential to weaken the current culture. It's crucial to integrate new hires and make sure they share the company's values.

Leadership Strain: It might be challenging for leadership teams to concentrate on cultural efforts when they are overworked. Leadership support and communication must be consistent.

Changes to Processes and Systems: Introducing new procedures and frameworks may cause a disruption in long-standing cultural norms and customs. Effective change management is essential.

Methods for Maintaining Culture and Morals

It takes intentional methods to preserve and nurture culture and values in a proactive manner:

Clear Vision and Values: Clearly state the mission, vision, and basic values of the organization. Make sure these are conveyed clearly and supported by decisions and actions.

Leadership Example: Culture is shaped and preserved in large part by leaders. Set a good example by acting in a way that embodies the principles and values of the organization.

Cultural Ambassadors: Find and give authority to cultural ambassadors inside the company. These people can support and uphold cultural norms within teams and geographical areas.

Onboarding and Training: Create thorough onboarding and training curricula that highlight the values and culture of the organization. Make certain that newly hired staff members comprehend and uphold these values.

Staff Engagement: Promote staff involvement through consistent correspondence, channels of feedback, and initiatives for employee recognition. Encourage staff members to actively participate in cultural projects by involving them.

Consistent Communication: Retain open and honest communication regarding cultural norms, objectives, and successes. Reach every employee, no matter where they are located, by using a variety of methods.

Recognition and Rewards: Acknowledge and honor actions that are consistent with the principles of the organization. Honor cultural accomplishments and anniversaries to promote constructive conduct.

Adaptability and Flexibility: Be willing to modify cultural norms to accommodate a varied and expanding workforce, all the while upholding your basic beliefs. Be open to suggestions and eager to make changes.

Best Practices and Case Studies

Gaining knowledge from the experiences of other businesses can be a great way to maintain culture while expanding.

Case Study Analysis: Examine case studies of businesses that have effectively preserved their cultures in the face of fast expansion. List the main tactics and methods they employed.

Best Practices: Implement best practices for maintaining cultural diversity, including frequent cultural evaluations, employee satisfaction surveys, and cross-functional team projects.

Continuous Improvement: Evaluate and refine cultural projects on a regular basis. To find areas that need improvement and make sure there is continuous cultural alignment, use performance measurements and feedback.

Businesses may sustain a coherent and positive corporate climate during periods of rapid development by proactively controlling culture and values. An effective cultural plan must have clear communication, a model of leadership, employee participation, and flexibility.

Managing Uncertainty and Change

Fast expansion frequently results in major uncertainty and upheaval. Navigating these difficulties and directing the organization through changes require effective leadership. This chapter will look at ways to build resilience, stay focused on long-term objectives, and lead through change and uncertainty.

The Character of Uncertainty and Change

Uncertainty and change are inevitable components of corporate expansion. They may originate from a number of sources, such as:

Market Dynamics: Uncertainty can arise from changes in the competitive environment, consumer preferences, and market conditions.

Internal Changes: Uncertainty and disruption to established routines might result from organizational reorganization, new procedures, and leadership changes.

External Factors: New possibilities and challenges may arise as a result of legislative changes, economic fluctuations, and technological breakthroughs.

Capabilities of a Leader to Manage Change

Successful leaders have particular traits that help them deal with uncertainty and change:

Vision and Clarity: Future-focused leaders need to articulate their vision clearly and effectively. Clarity gives the organization direction and aids in organizational alignment.

Adaptability: The capacity to change course and adjust tactics is essential. Leaders need to be adaptable and receptive to fresh perspectives.

Resilience: Leaders with resilience can overcome obstacles and setbacks. They keep a cheerful disposition and give others confidence.

Sympathy: It's critical to comprehend and respond to employees' worries and feelings. Leaders with empathy create a helpful environment and increase trust.

Decisiveness: It's critical to make prompt, well-informed decisions. Leaders with decisiveness are able to manage uncertainty and offer stability.

Communication: During times of transition,

effective communication is essential. Transparency in information delivery, active listening, and open communication are requirements for leaders.

Techniques for Taking Charge of Change

It takes a strategic approach and a focus on important areas to lead through change.

Change Management Strategy: Construct a thorough strategy, including the goals, procedures, and roles associated with the change endeavor. Accountability and clarity are ensured by an organized approach.

Involvement of Stakeholders: Reach out to stakeholders at all levels to win their cooperation and support. Engage partners, consumers, staff members, and investors in the process of change.

Communication Strategy: To ensure that everyone is informed, put in place a strong communication strategy. Make sure your messaging is consistent across channels. Respond to queries and give frequent updates.

Employee Support: Offer guidance, resources, and training to staff members. Assist them in comprehending the rationale behind the changes and how they will benefit the organization as a whole.

Participation and Empowerment: Encourage staff members to actively participate in the change process. Promote involvement and constructive criticism to cultivate a feeling of responsibility and dedication.

Monitoring and Evaluation: Track the development of change projects and assess their results. Utilize feedback and performance data to pinpoint areas that need work and make the required corrections.

Strengthening the Organization

The capacity to adjust and prosper in the face of uncertainty and change is known as organizational resilience. Developing resilience entails:

Building Core Capabilities: Make investments in enhancing fundamental skills like creativity, adaptability, and customer-focused ness. Robust skills facilitate the organization's ability to adapt to changes efficiently.

Cultivating a Positive Culture: Promote cooperation, education, and flexibility by fostering a positive and encouraging culture. A culture that is resilient can overcome obstacles and promote ongoing development.

Scenario Planning: Create a plan for imagining possible outcomes and obstacles. Create backup plans to handle unforeseen circumstances and guarantee readiness.

Encouraging Innovation: Promote an innovative work environment where staff members are encouraged to try new things, take chances, and come up with solutions. Growth and adaptation are fueled by innovation.

Leadership Development: To enhance the competencies of present and future leaders, fund initiatives that foster leadership. Navigating unpredictability requires effective leadership.

Best Practices and Case Studies

Gaining knowledge from other companies' experiences can give you important tips for navigating change and uncertainty as a leader:

Case Study Analysis: Examine case studies of businesses that have handled big transitions and unpredictabilities well. List the main tactics and approaches they employed as leaders.

Best Practices: Implement top techniques in

communication, staff engagement, and change management. To find areas that need work, compare your company to those that are successful.

Continuous Learning: Promote ongoing education and growth within the company. Keep up with developments in developing best practices, leadership techniques, and industry trends.

Businesses can successfully handle change and uncertainty by cultivating strong leadership traits, putting effective change management tactics into practice, and strengthening organizational resilience. In times of change, vision, flexibility, resilience, and good communication are essential elements of a successful leader.

CONCLUSION

Growing a company from $1 million to $10 million is a noteworthy achievement that calls for careful planning, unwavering execution, and fortitude in the face of difficulty. We have covered a variety of tactics and best practices for effectively growing your company in this book. Let's review the most important lessons learned as we come to an end and discuss the next steps to grow your company.

Important Lessons

1. **Assess Your Readiness:** Determine if your company is ready to scale before starting the process. To find areas that need improvement, assess your team's competencies, systems, procedures, and infrastructure.

2. **Define Your Vision:** Clearly state your objectives for growth. When navigating the challenges of development, having a clear direction and purpose helps you make the right choices and take the right actions.

3. **Build a Strong Foundation:** Make investments in scalable systems, procedures, and a healthy workplace culture to lay the groundwork for future development. Having a solid foundation means that your company will be able to handle the pressures of growing.

4. **Pay Attention to Leadership and Team Development:** Create a management structure and leadership team that are scalable to promote development. Make an investment in attracting, keeping, and

nurturing elite personnel who share your vision and principles.

5. **Create Sturdy Sales and Marketing Plans:** Increase the size of your marketing campaigns to attract new audiences and grow your clientele. To increase sales, put in place effective sales procedures and make use of technology.

6. **Streamline Operations and Enhance Efficiency:** By putting in place effective systems, procedures, and financial planning, you may scale your operations. Continuous expansion requires efficient cash flow management.

7. **Identify Growth Opportunities:** Keep an eye out for chances for growth, strategic alliances, and new markets. Mergers and acquisitions, among other strategic

development activities, may hasten your journey to $10 million.

8. **Maintain Focus on Culture and Values:** As your company expands, continue to protect and cultivate its culture and values. Long-term success, customer happiness, and staff engagement are all enhanced by a strong culture.

9. **Lead Through Change and Uncertainty:** To successfully manage change and uncertainty, hone your leadership skills. Develop organizational resilience to handle changing market circumstances and obstacles.

Subsequent Actions to Expand Your Enterprise

Consider Your Professional Path: Spend some time appreciating your accomplishments and thinking back on your company experience so far. Acknowledge the strides you have made and the challenges you have overcome.

Evaluate Your Progress: Assess your development in relation to your objectives and aims for scaling. Determine your strengths and opportunities for development.

Create a Scaling Plan: Create a thorough scaling plan that details your goals, deadlines, and next actions based on your evaluation. For successful progress tracking, break down your objectives into smaller, more achievable milestones.

Implement Continuous Improvement: Encourage your company to adopt a culture of continuous improvement. To promote development and innovation, promote learning at all levels, creativity, and feedback.

Invest in Your Team: Make an investment in

the training and development of your staff and leadership group. Offer prospects for advancement, education, and proficiency enhancement to cultivate a proficient and driven labor force.

Remain Agile and Adaptive: Keep your scaling strategy flexible and adaptable. Be prepared to adjust your tactics, try out novel concepts, and act fast on opportunities and changes in the market.

Monitor and measure performance: To keep an eye on your development and output, set up key performance indicators (KPIs). To remain on track to reach your $10 million objective, analyze your KPIs on a regular basis and make any adjustments to your plans.

Remain Dedicated to Your Goals: As you advance, don't waver from your goals and principles. Even in the midst of difficulties and uncertainty, let them direct your choices and actions.

Celebrate Successes and Learn from Failures: Acknowledge and take lessons from your mistakes as well as your accomplishments. As a company leader, both achievements and setbacks teach you important lessons that advance your career.

Seek Support and Guidance: Don't be afraid to ask advisers, mentors, and business specialists for help and direction. Have a network of reliable advisers around you to help you overcome the challenges of growth. They can provide advice and insights.

To sum up, growing your company from $1 million to $10 million is a difficult but worthwhile process. You may attain sustainable development and create a flourishing company that leaves a lasting impression by putting the tactics and best practices in this book into practice while remaining true to your vision and core principles. Recall that scaling involves more than simply hitting a revenue target; it also entails adding value, helping clients, and changing the world. Thus, go on with self-assurance, resolve, and an unwavering commitment to quality. Your path to $10 million begins right now.

www.ingramcontent.com/pod-product-compliance
Lightning Source LLC
Chambersburg PA
CBHW050059230526
45470CB00004B/1591